UNRAVELING AT THE NAME

Unraveling at the Name

JENNY FACTOR

 Copper Canyon Press

Grateful acknowledgment is made to James Moore for the use of his painting *White Calla Lily* on the cover. Thanks also to Schmidt-Bingham Gallery.

The author also wishes to thank Paul Asimow, Herbert Barg, Marilyn Hacker, Sam Hamill, and Copper Canyon Press.

Copper Canyon Press is in residence under the auspices of the Centrum Foundation at Fort Worden State Park in Port Townsend, Washington. Centrum sponsors artist residencies, education workshops for Washington State students and teachers, blues, jazz, and fiddle tunes festivals, classical music performances, and The Port Townsend Writers' Conference.

LIBRARY OF CONGRESS
CATALOGING-IN-PUBLICATION DATA
Factor, Jenny, 1969–
Unraveling at the name / by Jenny Factor.
    p. cm.
ISBN 1-55659-176-4 (alk. paper)
1. Lesbians—Poetry. 1. Title.
PS3606.A26 U57 2002
811'.6—DC21   2001007422

9 8 7 6 5 4 3 2 FIRST PRINTING
COPPER CANYON PRESS
Post Office Box 271
Port Townsend, Washington 98368
www.coppercanyonpress.org

For Myra Cohn Livingston
(1926–1996)

2001 HAYDEN CARRUTH AWARD

The Hayden Carruth Award was established in 1998 to honor the most distinguished first, second, or third book manuscript from among more than one thousand entries received at Copper Canyon Press.

ACKNOWLEDGMENTS

Grateful acknowledgment is made to the journals and publications in which many of these poems, some in slightly different form, are forthcoming or have appeared:

"Going Down" appeared in *Not for the Academy: Lesbian Poets,* edited by Lilian Mohin (London: Onlywomen Press, 1999).

"Canzone" appeared in *Nerve* (www.nerve.com) (August 2001).

"Conciliation" and "Mating of Horseshoe Crabs" appeared in *Harrington Lesbian Fiction Quarterly* (fall 2001).

"A High Cold Bright Full Moon" and "Custody or Visitation" appeared in *PN Review* (January–February 2001).

"Extramarital..." appeared in *Nerve* (www.nerve.com) (April 2000).

"Happenstance" appeared in *Shenandoah* (fall 1999).

"Learning Stick" appeared in *Prairie Schooner* (summer 2001).

"Mermaid's Wedding License" and "Unrequited Love" appeared in *Epoch* (fall 2000).

"Sonnet" appeared in *Ploughshares* (April 2001).

"To Twenty Canada Geese in the Palisades Industrial Park" appeared in *The Paris Review* (winter 2001).

If I am not for myself, who will be for me?
If I am only for myself, who am I?
And if not now, when?

Rabbi Akiba

CONTENTS

One

CONCILIATION

Good morning. If it is a good morning.
Which I doubt.
      Eeyore

The Eeyore glass, a family running joke,
from Sam's juice set with Tigger, Piglet, Pooh,
was mine last night. I set it for myself
beside the mat-less place he's led me to
since last week when he made off with my chair.
No question who is running this loose ship,
where parents jockey to get let off chores.
We're babies raising babies. That's a fact.
This marriage worked its best when we had time
to raise each other. Now we rock our pains
to sleep ourselves in beds on separate floors.
I dream of women, want a different life.
I backslid several weeks in just one night.

My after-meal design—a party north
of Houston, east of Fourth with writing friends.
Ben stopped by while I dressed so he could mope
about our pain in company. Then I
got caught in traffic on 9A, sat trapped
until my aisle of autos in reverse
backed down an entry ramp past two police.
(The world stood on its head.) I double-parked,
ran up to say hello then moved the car
to some dark one-way road off Bleecker Street.
(Did bumper grind to squeeze into the spot.)
Then went upstairs, knew no one, poured a drink,
took off my coat, felt lost, and found the john.
I peed, picked up my coat, and left again.

Went driving heading north and fingered thoughts
that wove between the wails of Ani di
singing out her love for some man's wife.
I tried to find a way to write my life
with staying married in it, but I couldn't.
Each option looked like death. A Stepford wife
is what Ben says he would not want again:
the days immobilized by doubt and ill
self-definition, I lay flat and read,
a poet-writer who couldn't pen a word
for several years as soon as we were wed,
but still could talk philosophy *à table*.
We knew I was depressed but didn't know why:
an energy turned inward, dammed up.

                                        Red
of traffic lights and tail lights pierced my car.
Wrote letters in my head, they all began:
Believe no word I say after tonight.
I'm going back to sleep. Forget I'm gay.
I'll say I'm happy. Don't trust what I say.
And made a list of friends to send it to.
Then in the tangled mess where Broadway knots
itself 'round Lincoln Center hatched a plan:
to find a phone, call Erin in Vermont,
and drive four hours for a pity fuck.
I'd show up at her co-op where we'd talk
of summer nights spent groping until dawn,
her body casting moonlight. Then I'd hold
her, have my cry into her silent hair.

She'd send me home to Ben when we were done.
She likes Ben, but I love her far too well
to use our friendship as a scratching post.
And so I turned on Henry Hudson Park,
drove home along the dark throat of the PIP,
thinking, "This is hell. I live in it.
And what can my desire do with bars
and lists of women I don't really know?"
The scarves of fog swept in around my car.
My exit led me off into dense trees.
I turned toward home, nosing duly east.
When I got in, Sam, wrapped in father's arms,
was dozing off to Disney Sing-Along
well past eleven. Soft fluorescent hum.

We climbed the stairs. The TV crackled out.
Sam curled in bed, I gave Ben what he asked—
the change only semantic after all—
a backslide into language of the past:
an Open Marriage, not a Trial Divorce,
between a lesbian woman, a straight man
who cannot bear to hurt each other much.
So with a vow to make the best of it,
we tossed two hours in our separate beds
and for the first time in three distant weeks
ate family breakfast, let our glasses touch.

SUMMER JOURNAL, ISRAEL (AGE 19)

After work, we'll hit the kibbutz beach.
The whole group tans together, half-undressed.
I write it all in letters home to Lise:
My bunkmate, Val, might be a lesbian.
My keenest crush is Sean, an older man,
bandanna'd, dimpled chin, and cute, but married.

So horny-crazed, I bet I'll never marry;
that day we drink warm beers out on the beach —
Sean and I. A skinny Kenyan man
offers me ten dollars to undress
for him. Sure I could be a lesbian
but only if I were trying it with Lise.

I save each letter I get back from Lise.
One week, her roommate sophomore year gets married.
The next, she drives her aunt, a lesbian,
to the family cottage by the beach.
And do I have her new address?
And please do tell about those men!

And so I write her how a young French man —
brilliant, fine-boned, with an aunt named Lise —
and I went swimming naked. We undressed
under stars, butt-drunk and making merry,
among the jellyfish and wave-washed beach,
till Val came out and watched (that lesbian!).

Lise knows for certain she's no lesbian,
although she's never liked it with a man,
I tell Val as we walk out to the beach.
I'm sure Val must be gay, I write to Lise,
because she says she never wants to marry
and doesn't shave (I see when she's undressed).

The night Sean kissed me in my Spanish dress,
he said he used to date a lesbian
some years before he and his wife got married,
and once he'd even made love to a man!
We drank some Scotch. I showed him Lise's
picture. Our footprints watermarked the paper beach,

and then I wondered if I'd marry, beach,
reach shore? *Am I a lesbian? A man?*
Wind blew my dress. I stood. I thought of Lise.

TO TWENTY CANADA GEESE
IN THE PALISADES INDUSTRIAL PARK

Ladies, it is late. The lake is ice.
You've surely seen the heron fly beyond
the great black oak. And watched the robins go,
the nuthatch go, the koi pond crusted silver.

It's February in the yellowed grass.
Beneath the bones of trees: the sleeted pond.
Your broad feet tromp on wet dirt-seeded snow.
You stroll and browse for seeds — no thought of cover.

Making much of little, once or twice
a morning, you take flight in lines, you land
on littered lawns, then join a crowd, and slowly
start to eat and talk again. The ganders

have flown off. The day is nice.
Your chatter's feminine and frisky, fond
and fierce as fishwives gossiping at bowls
of snap peas or as women giving orders

in town square or at market haggling price.
In short, your calls are comfortable. You stand
your suffering in good company. You chose
the fate of any small group wintering over,

the long tradition of a well-shared strife,
the strength of staying on familiar ground.
Ladies, it is late and I am cold.
My hands are empty. Go and find another

to bread your windy sojourn on the ice.
Across the bridge above the frozen pond,
I make my way, a woman come alone
to where the grass is dead and there's no cover.

I choose the strangest spots to winter-over.

Rocking in a hammock after dark, head
full of tree. Moon trying to interject herself. Truly
summer. Did I, actually, see the green flash
of one firefly, first beneath me, then off
down the road? The neighbors opened
their sprinklers and served doughnuts
on the patio. In a bedroom above

the street, nap hour, between lips, I'd took
the smooth bulb again — inhaling wolf, boy, father,
the gray temple where I'd aged him,
small gray fur over an ear's tender
lobe, then beneath, his lips flat and sheened
like water, ready, unready for my explore,
stroke, suck. Each muscle smoothing back

under fingers like sand, his penis
obedient and shy, no, sly, a girl of a daisy
of an up-up shoot, under tongue under
fingertips, his shuddering, his sigh,
his there   and yes   and there
until I moistened and thickened between
thighs until I let his mouth

ride me with a flick flick higher, higher,
(our child's high snoring from the bunk next door),
the air sweat-sweet and the birdsong
glistening, dizzying, cascading, and I ready
to let him. This afternoon in that room.
Afterwards, giddy, we stood
to our uncomfortably disparate heights. He,

a man, smiling with the helpless metallic sunlight
of a summer car, while I rode out my woman's
vapor, found myself laughing like a lazy
dance of finches in our hawthorn tree. *Differences
worry me. Could I get used to them with this body's
languor?* Outside after, as he and our son
wheeled a truck down our block, I wondered

whether I should leave. He wondered
whether to hang the hammock, measured
and ratcheted it between solid trees. We three
lofted it up. Took turns. Swung.
After dark, I left them both inside and rocked
in that outside womb he bought in Mexico,
staring up into leaves. Suspended

over our block with the tricycles and the popsicles,
the grass clippings and the stroller wheels.
Did I, actually, see the green flash
of one firefly, first beneath me, then off
down the road? My head was full
of tree. And Moon popped through,
trying to interject herself. Naturally....

Scotch and Soda

The front door slipped from its latch and he
came in—the man you're married to and love.
He knows about this "us," this you-and-me,
and it is for his sake that words like "love"
and "tomorrow" don't flow between us easily;
when Ella slips into the groove on the CD
player, your shirt lifts above your head
(my ice settling in my glass, I feel sour beads
of sweat from the summer heat rising
on my skin). Here the truth is surprising
even to me: I don't mind what we *don't*
say, what you *can't* feel. "I love you" is scary.
I mean something lighter. What I want:
Lay with me, wide-eyed, wary.

Rubyfruit

You kissed my mouth as if it were my sex
before you kissed me everywhere, before
that night in Rubyfruit's, my glasses off,
the room elided, darkness stretched, a blur
zip-studded by red pinlights, hemmed and held
a cloth we had no future written on.
Around us, well-dressed women stirred the darkness
as they walked. The bar's cold black streak streamed
past willows, necks swayed in to sup and speak.
I learned the map of textures on your cheek.
Benched near the place where others knit limbs, lives,
my body's affirmation—a surprise—
to our established friendship. You confessed—
amazing humming of my flesh's yes.

Playing Doctor

Yes, my love, I'm yours. I'll give myself
over to your teasing, tender care
to let you open me, deliberate,
your hand, a scientist, whose probing dares
to peel the blossom budded thirty years
in silence. I wake like a newborn, tears
of trust and outrage, wet and cold and bared.
What will be born of us when you have dared
to lift my fetal, embryonic heat
toward your nipples on my floral sheets?
What climax will our drumming raise us toward?
When we make love, new love, what will be made?
In that place, exposed, exhausted, laid,
if I'm with you, I will not feel afraid.

"Now What Can We Do for My Pretty?" You Ask....

Sometimes I touch my breasts and think of you.
Sometimes, as if my body were your own
private kingdom, I don't want my own
hands to touch myself after you
leave the room. It's like you lock me from myself
by going away. Inside my insides,
I am half-awake, half-opened. From your side
of New York, the Great Woods, you check your shelf
for potions, ivories, hairpieces, sleek combs
to knit my hair around when you return.
Oh mistress, busy worldly woman, turn
the bolt; return to me; set your combed
nape in my lap. Kiss me till the fine
evening turns a deep flush, like your skin, mine.

Misapprehension

I don't want you always to act your age:
Fall apart a little for me, please,
so when I kiss your mouth, your brow, your creamy
arms, your downy neck, eyelids, your strange
intense dark copper-lidded eyes that close
against me, when I hold you till your whole
strut-length of spine releases to my holding,
when I lay you, stroke your guiltless rose
open toward me, ages overturned...
I don't want you to act your age, just yearn
toward what I offer; soften to my touch,
let me reach the place where you give milk,
suck and tongue you till my touch is much,
much more than youth or age or silk on silk.

Adrift

Curled up in my arms like a small boy,
you took my breast into your hungry lips
and met my eye and smiled, nursing child,
and cried into my lap when you had come
too many times for your skin to endure
more touch, and cried and cried till you were done
while I said, *Si si si,* as to my son's
despondent nighttime-waking. Dream-wracked, dear,
your rosy body swam through sweetness, tears
on the black sheets of your bed in the ambient light
of two candles. Like a ship sailing to a shore
we've never reached before, we sailed each other
leg over leg, your back washed up against my breasts
till your son's door opened and we dressed.

Safer Sex?

So no more nipples? (Post-lactation leak.)
And winter comes like sandpaper to lips
which now keep their chaste distance from my lips.
Of course my palm may stroke your nether cheek
as long as I wear gloves for full descent
into the place you want my dig and thrust.
Sex, you call this. I say, lack of trust.
You say I'm inching toward an argument.
I call your latex, Safe Sex for the Heart.
I want to find your mouth on me, the taste
of you, familiar, moving with my tongue.
You've come. Neglected, handled, and unstrung,
I stay in bed and watch you dress in haste.
I've lost more than one sense without your taste.

Confidential P.S.

So now when we make love, what have we made?
Not "life," although our blossoming belies
a simple definition of mere breath
and heartbeat. Surely something is implied
we do not make: not home, not spouse, not child
(though sometimes I am yours or you are mine
in ways that seem to posit us *en womb*).
When others speak of loving to create
a life, we know we'll never share a room
for more than hours running. Yes. I mind
this making time by time and lay by lay
a stay against the current of our days.
Real work that moves no rivers. Mother, wife,
we live out elsewhere. Love knitting no life.

HAPPENSTANCE

My neighbors' garden's shaped by oddball love:
spare tires planted with hibiscus blooms,
a fairy circle sprouting up in bulbs,
the grass a mass of weeded happenstance.

Spare tires — planted with hibiscus — bloom
like perfect testaments to making-use,
while grass, a weeded mass, by happenstance
pops up white and purple pixie heads.

Like perfect testaments to making-use,
nests fill night lanterns, nesting boxes, trees.
Newborn sparrows lift their pixie heads.
A little boy runs through a square of reeds.

Nests fill night lanterns, nesting boxes, trees.
Fecundity is everywhere I look.
A little boy runs through a square of reeds
as if he's acting out a children's book.

Fecundity is everywhere I look.
Good use is made of every accident
in family-planted gardens. Children's books
are seldom whimsy-riddled as these nooks.

Good use. How can they make of accident
a happy beauty? I am so confused.
Whimsy poses riddles in these nooks.
Life's not about what's given, but what's used.

Such happy beauty leaves me here, confused
inside a fairy circle made of bulbs:
my life — much given, sometimes little used,
set in this garden, shaped by oddball love.

Ten crazy minutes when it almost worked:
from bedtime crackers, Sam and I segued
to playing, singing terse Cole Porter songs
(Cole smiling cross-legged on the frontispiece,
queer and dapper; married, as I am),
and Ben, who can't bear eighth notes poorly swung—
an amateur musician, nearly pro—
laid off his book and sat down at the keys.
I swept and scooped our son across the floor
while gender-bending lyrics, sotto voiced.
Then Ben stopped playing, taught me how to lead
left foot, right foot, til our feet agreed,
"Night and Day," "I Happen To Like New York."

What did they do, that late and earnest autumn
the child moved to the center of their bed?
Like a stone in a pond's silence, his tiny
heartbeat pulsing out a mood of fragileness
all along the old wall-to-wall carpet.
His decibel, a teapot's, sometimes endless,
heated by precisely what flame?
Neither had the will to put him back.
His body became like a familiar argument,
an unshakable consciousness, resting
happily in the quick cream of his mother's breath
while the maple tree outside their window ripened,
whispering, "Descant. Descent. Disconnect."

Sometimes she would slam the refrigerator door
and look around at the juice spilled on the floor
and her son's criminal's guilt and feel as if she were
a panther ready to murder when it can't run
from its cage. Sometimes she would be
so exhausted by her own rage she would look for
any place to rest. But there was no place
entirely hers left. The child filled out space
like inkiness. Sometimes she was glad
to see the child cry, feeling, righteously, Life isn't fair.
On long days when she was alone with that wide-eyed
witness, she wanted her friend, his other thoughts
close to hers. Other thought closed from her.

Is love a liability in parenthood? Surely
the baby in the first crisis of sensation
doesn't care about anyone's exhaustion
or despair. Ministering to the first slap
of World against iridescent eyelids,
one has no use for the discussion of equals,
comrades sharing their kitchen, world-
sphere. And who had ever seen so many
hours stitched together, laid out beside one another,
to move through as through pond water?
And the ancient Man and ancient Woman
called up where two children once romped
and wrapped legs around each other.

He held the small boy on the couch
while the doctor clipped the thin stitches
on his chin. If he could have made that
tiny metaphor painless, he would have,
but knew of no escape from the chasm of
a living room a child is bleeding in,
as a pin sutures what was born
perfectly made. Tearless, the child closes
his eyes in trust, white-lipped, afraid.
So the father wraps his arms around
the little braveness that is him, and Him,
and ultimately, himself: a child's back pressed
to a man's frightened, furiously pounding chest.

When they stood together outside a concert
or the school principal's office, he had nothing
to say in the silence, and she would try to speak
the way she couldn't when the child was there.
Released back into their two-ness, her voice
pinched up inside her, tightened up
threadbare, riding out familiar rhythms
she felt that she had drunk up from some well
she had no business dipping in.
And sometimes she would dream
she heard another voice like an angel's,
ungendered, human, fiercely anchored.
It was hers. It was also hers.

In the creep of early morning she could
carry friendship to her ear, the phone crooning words
into her, then laughter. Then she'd believe
in change again, in transformation. The houseplants
blossoming on their green lungs, and in the bedroom
two roots, sunk deeper into dreams. Through
that much space, world gleamed. Surely a family is
a multiheaded organism that feels only
what it can share. Is there some ancient lesson in
curtailed individual sensation? Life piquing
through a screen? And when one's own head
is no more than a limb? Is there some valuable lesson then?
What creeps like ivy over the fence into the yards of neighbors?

The boy became a backyard window watcher
as Night laid its shadow on the garden,
closed each pebble in its hand, and stilled
the grassy lawn. He'd look out on a foggy
morning to a world gone white, see the scuffle,
the fight that brings each brown leaf down,
while trees struggled in their yoke of bone,
and the thin ficus snapped, tumbling the flower pots.
Only he'd know where the black cat likes to go.
And when the rain would land in the pool like frogs,
water circling outward over the rim, he'd stare
waiting late through the glass, cold pane pressed to ear,
listening, when all that's left to do is hear.

The contract signed, the seawitch bid me sing
in that dark cave where closed anemones
held souls in fingered palms. The waves beat on
silently to those flecked distant shores
that I was heading toward. I knew it now.
I felt the hard knot of my voice, the click
unlatched into the currents of the cave.
I sang, I sang. As if my ribs were notes.
Inside that vale of voice, the sweet hard ache
let go like fists, a hundred open doors.
I'd never heard my sound so clear before.
My voice flew out of me to fill the cup
of Nothingness the seawitch held high up.
I woke in stabbing light, on solid ground,
then died or wed, both stories are the same,
for in the act of love where tangled legs
move me to tears, I can't call any name.

UNRAVELING AT THE NAME

1

The first time I was kissed I was sixteen,
under bottle brushes at the park,
red, stunted kisses, backed against the bark,
our Pesach picnic rained on at our feet.
Jeff, broad around as dad to a small child,
ran sausage fingers through my frizzing hair.
A tingling started in my underwear.
I caught scared shivers, shaking till we piled
into his flat suburban, where he turned
on heat and radio and rubbed his hands
along my arms and legs. His kisses mild
and numbly kind as dad's. His heavy eyes
searched mine, his glasses off. My stomach soured,
but shaking slowed. He kissed me there for hours.

2

That Sunday, under sheets stitched with my name,
I played the day again, and turned the dial
to find Bruce Springsteen singing "I'm On Fire"
once more on the clock radio by the narrow
bed I slept in. I thought I'd caught the flu.
I might have, for the way my stomach lurched
each time I passed my parents in the den.
Their TV show, a game of cat and mouse
between a bicepsed man and a high-heeled blonde
whose hungering eyes I noticed first that day.
So this was what the world was doing when
I read *Jane Eyre* and learned to play Chopin!
I stroked my nightgown feeling oddly sick,
spread-eagled on the bed, finger to tit.

3

My shaking slowed. We'd stayed parked several hours
then turned the car west, heading for the pier
at sunset, where the circus atmosphere —
bumper cars, a Ferris wheel, the powder
pink of cotton candy, shouts of children —
made us feel old and wise. He told me how
his college applications had gone out
to schools with novelists. His glasses glinting
thick and serious, his fierce wet mouth
in search of mine until I could not breathe.
By dark we left the pier to find the beach,
his thick hand on my small one. We climbed out
and laid on sand. I mused, *So this is what
a woman feels: warm winds, insistent mouth.*

4

Spread-eagled on the bed, finger to tit,
my high school years — a lonely wash of wants —
I dreamed of being dragged into my skin
by some sarcastic boy who made remarks,
of sucking off my brilliant best guy friend,
tonguing down his eager daunting shaft
(I saw one in a *Playgirl* photograph,
flaccid but long). Sex seemed a way to kneel.
I loved male power, tried to hide my own.
Few hints I might be homosexual:
no thoughts of sex before I turned sixteen.
I had a recurring harem fantasy,
my gender made strange changes in my dreams.
And one night in college at the Blarney Stone.

5

I've learned the way a woman feels: her mouth
is lighter than a man's. The taste of her
is sweeter, even after onion soup.
Spread-eagled on the bed, finger to tit,
the taste of her is fine. My tongue set loose
finding where she wants me, sucking her,
my hand inside her. What a spot that is.
My pinkie on the silk around her anus.
How she arches, pelvis lifts. She laughs,
sunflowers in her eyes. After, she smiles
like every seagull flapping wings at once
and taking off. My college fantasies
of Lise, my dearest friend, were chaste—just this:
dry months, I'd fall asleep, dream of her kiss.

6

After six shots each at the Blarney Stone
I tottered seven long Manhattan blocks
with Sandy to the Harvard Club. In socks,
inside the ladies' restroom, with toothbrush
while other women washed up, Sandy called
me over, paused, and kissed me quizzically.
Then on the Weld Room's ancient crimson rug
(where Lise and others slept off hangovers),
swelled secrets in our sleeping bags, we kissed,
stroked hands and faces, hoping no one saw.
Her kisses slipped in quickly, satin-soft
surprise of sweetness, seemed light as a joke.
Near dawn, we stumbled silent to the bus:
soppy, tender, headachy, still buzzed.

7

Before the sleeping bags, after the kissing,
Sandy whispered that we had to talk.
So holding soap in plastic case, we took
the back stairs to the locker rooms that top
the Harvard Club. The hiss of water filled
the shower stall. I watched her well-shaved form
in shiny suds. She whispered, *With my boyfriends*
or alone — I've never come. The Ivory
scent desexualized her teasing talk.
I watched the flash of orange pubic hair
and wondered if I wanted her. The steam
beat at the yellow lights flecked with winged moths,
her lathered skin, a marble draped in scarves.
Would I? airborne, still a question mark.

8

Soppy-tender, street-singing, abuzz,
my friend Lise and I left Z-Bar, then wandered
through new Leverett Quad, across the lawn
cut by a moonlit walkway. Her dark head
haloed from the streetlamps' fairy globes.
She said, *C'm'ere,* and lay down on the grass.
I went to her. Raspberry scent of lotion,
her voice, low muted, chimed, *Now let's be sponges*
soaking stars. So we turned up our palms
and filled with sky. The blackness held its breath.
How deep I loved her intellect, her
silliness. Grass in her hair, she tasted leaves
off down the block. I watched her through pine trees,
my hazy lashes studding her in stars.

9

Would I? airborne, still a question mark,
I set out to lose my virginity —
a college freshman — quite deliberately,
with Ben, a tall kind scientist my age
who played his flute at midnight, measured bars
of Mozart in his eyes. I liked sex more
than kissing; all the textures — scrotum, cock,
warmth rising in our raw and tender spots.
That flowered spring we skipped classes to stroke
each other on the lawn, sun on our limbs.
The year I fell for Lise I still loved him,
and loved him after Sandy on the bus
quit my row to eat lunch in the back.
She called me *sick,* my body, *horrible.*

10

Ann's brilliant eyelashes studded with tears,
on the bench outside the science wing
in high school, her lips trembling as she talked
(*If I were a man, I'd kiss her now,* I'd thought);
or Dale's wrestler-like bounce as he skip-walked
along the hall, tapping locker doors;
the hawks and sunlight in Melissa's eyes;
the scar that curled near Julie's pubic bone,
white on blue veins the year before she died;
Lynn's dyed-black flip, her sassy tattooed arms;
the soupy tenderness of Sara's smile;
tall horsey Mary with her sturdy neck;
Ben at his math, square jaw intensely still:
Bodies, bodies — aren't they beautiful?

11

Inside the body, something horrible
is waiting to get out. Ask any child.
The dreadful urgency of appetite
unrecognized. Excretion grown-ups miss
or rip us from our playing to wipe off.
Ignored desire seems our own bad fault.
First angers rise, our lashing-out small palms
start slapping with the normal recompense:
sad solitude in some dark room. Our song
can make our mother stop the car to shout.
For those of us who have an awful love,
ungainly, overeager, and does not fit
inside the shape our friendships offer it,
a history emerges. We "come out."

12

Aging bodies are so beautiful.
Secure in age, my eyes stop editing
stretch marks, square hands, my masculinity,
the spreading breadth of hips. Then suddenly
I start to look at Love, one weekend with
a friend I love. She says, *Cyrano for
Roxanne felt love like sunrise summoning
the best in him; while Tristan and Isolde
loved shadows in each other, circled death.*
We need more words for love, so we define
the fullest loves we've felt. I come alive:
there's woman after woman, count the names.
Stretched near her dreaming, I cry half the night,
a happy fire in my body's home.

13

Ungainly truths get trimmed for history:
When Sandy kissed me, I thought, *Is this all?*
The kisses seem too slippery, too soft.
I need my love more solid, difficult.
When Jeff first kissed me, stomach-sick, aroused,
I lay in bed all night and stroked my tit.
After Sandy's kiss, the next weekday,
I joined the college BGLSA.
We love where we must learn: I've loved a woman
like my father, a man who cradled me
till dawn; my love, a muscled poetry
for my best friend. *Our sexuality*
takes form only through some interpreting:
The sheet's stitching unravels at the name.

14

On the radio, Bruce Springsteen sings
"I'm On Fire," to a girl at home
alone, a song about his bad desire.
In bed, I touch myself. Fixed to that fire,
I weigh and measure all my dreams of sex.
Quiet. In the stillness: nudity.
I watch my costume fall, my skins and gauze.
I want to touch as if there were no laws.
Slip softly from your clothes and come to me.
I promise not to yield or overpower.
I'll tell you stories honest as my name
and listen to yours till our eyes are moons,
until the World looks whole. When dawn's red lifts
I'll kiss you like the first time you were kissed.

15

Under bottle brushes I was kissed
and slept in sheets with someone else's name.
I shook, but shaking slowed in several hours
spread-eagled on the bed, finger to tit.

So this is how a woman feels, I thought
after six shots each at the Blarney Stone.
In sleeping bags, we groped after the kisses:
soppy, tender, headachy, still buzzed.

Who am I? airborne, quite a question mark.
Her silent eyelashes, studded with tears.
My body's yearning, strange and horrible;
her body beautiful as coming home.

My story's underneath this history.
Turn off the radio. I want to sing.

MATING OF HORSESHOE CRABS

Like fallen moons,
leather purses,
metals tumbled by the sea,
they blink the air in dazedly
along the arc of beach.
Then clumsy, slowly lumbering,
they somehow move their shells aside
so that one can get inside
the ample body of the other.
Then they lie on the pebbled sheet,
shocked by the tender glowing place
beneath the battered surfaces,
the ocean's raw white flesh.
And then they go,
stacked crab boats,
tails slicing in the tide,
pushing off, adrift,
they ride the foamy currents
out so deep
that from my shore
I cannot see
the moment of unjoining.
How often have I gone in early morning
looking for the crabs in April winds?
How often have I reached a gentle finger
toward some beautiful shelled creature,
searching for the tender place,
the part that opens,
wanting till I cannot breathe
that slow joined ride
in ocean?

Two

This morning every parked car bathes in snow.
Last night I ambled through a grimy rain
twenty blocks to home from the last metro's
premature "Get off." A broken train

unstitched my evening's end, while more numb rain
bleach-washed my thought, returning from a slow
dinner party, coat-wrapped, tense-lipped, strained
two-week-old separated, finally solo,

a single silent woman searching Ninth who
found her buzzer, climbed an endless stair.
Like college, coat piled on a pile of coats.
No proof I'm wife or mother otherwhere.

I'd met the guests I did not know—men—trained
myself to conversation though my throat
closed up. I managed wine, and half a plate
of couscous in a fruit sauce, hugged my host

and chatted with an old friend whom I snowed
in questions to block questions. Debonair
and polished, she showed her decade of self-growth
while I'd pushed prams. My new flat's dust-ball bare.

Then premature "Get off," a broken train
twenty blocks from home, where no metro
would take me. All the way in grimy rain,
I walked to sleep; till dawn came dove-gray. Snow.

The lemon tree squat & sweet.
Wings scuffling into the eaves.
Bird eyes peek from the roof.
Parenting's own coffin.

How jolly for the little fellows,
feathered eyeless thumbs
who are birthed where I cannot rest
and call my roof their home.

Where I live is a hole:
lack of people, dis-ease.
But up in the great crowding:
tightness and the pleasing.

The wood is more real for defining
with beaten wings the trap,
for nesting in the tightness
and never trying a latch.

SONNET

There were lies. You knew, but then forgot
the child peeking around the corner, hiding
from you. Wind sifts through the beechnut
arbor. Peripheral, the real story goes trailing
moonlike, behind the car window, just beyond
view. And how bad is it to have believed the best
of your story, or a lover's; to have rested
in that sweetness that is sweetest
when forgot: a dog's head on your lap, fuchsia blooming
in a pot, whether tended to or not? Now the child
in the closet wonders (frightened, cold)
if the darkness will lift before dinner. *Hold
out your hands, Mother,* he thinks, hoping.
The door swings open. The face is wild.

Today I'm Under Construction and
can hardly circumnavigate my brain

without running into orange cones.
This makes driving in the City quite a challenge,

alone with myself in a locked car, no place to go,
damned traffic report blaring on the radio:

"Pipework on Agape Street. A hotspot in the vicinity
of Occupation. Expect twenty-minute delays

in Self-Esteem. Head-on collision
at the intersection of Child Custody and Visitation.

Sig Alert in Digestion; had to completely
shut down Sleep." So don't expect an easy answer,

no immediate delivery. I'm stuck on the highway
in heavy traffic, wrapped in internal debate

and making my slow way toward Greenwich
Street. I may be impossibly late.

If anybody errs, it will be you.
Don't tell me stories that later you'll deny,
or brag of your affairs now that we're through.
I only told you what you asked me to.
Would you prefer that I recant or lie
when everything you heard is true?
If anybody errs, it will be you.
What crime could I be charged with in reply?
I told you just what you asked me to.
If anybody errs, it will be you.
Not I. Not I. Not I. Not I. Not I.

Lingering glances, tender kisses
didn't yield sex in February
despite abundant sweet near-misses.

Surely Valentine's Day bliss is—
listen to this Visionary—
a chance for lingering glances, kisses

but cruel Cupid's dreadful trick is
each cold dawn lifts solitary
over my February misses.

Bold acts went less well than wishes.
I'd have saved face if more wary.
Love declared before the kisses

led my Lady onto disses.
I *might* have let my hot eyes tarry
on the buns of sweet near Misses.

not expended angst on vicious
unrequited heat, to parry
lingering glances, dim-lit kisses.

I'd get more sex at average brisses,
where all women seem more merry
than She whose glances nixed my kisses
to spite the plans of this ex-Mrs.

Boys are all right. I have a thing for *girls*
Their dresses are a festive celebration.

Silk or flannel, girls are what I *like*
My vice acts out in any situation.

One glance at women's hands is liable *to*
tumble me toward vain infatuation.

A girl's jeans zipper beckons me to *pull*
and coax the tongue to fabric separation.

I'm partial to girls' napes of necks and *their*
haircuts, long or short. Each alteration

causes fresh astonishment. Short *skirts* —
their skittish hemlines dance a demarcation

summoning my eyes to follow *down*
the length of leg, imagine exploration

with tongue and lips and hands. I would far *rather*
soft upper arms, light licks, the levitation

of thin hairs in a breeze on calves and nipples *than*
waste my tongue in witty conversation.

So Woman let your blue eyes throw me *over*
leonine and slow. This titillation

must lead to yes and yes and there and *their*
to skin on skin with no more hesitation

as hot tongues tease two shy and slippery *heads!*
to healthy heat. Sing praise! Sing exultation!

Look, child, I should have mentioned this before.
You're almost four years old. I didn't think—
or should have realized you were noticing,
all your years of watching. So now, look,
my son, and see how beautiful we are!
In Central Park today the sun's unlocked
the gates of joy, and let loose on the lawn
the people. There's a sound of hop and horn.
And every sprinkler has street-worshippers.
Walking through West Harlem, how you laughed

when those three girls hosed our fleeing fleet,
calling, "You go, Girl," "That boy's a peach."
The corners seemed to smoke with pressed-up heat.
Perhaps I should have named our differences:
The woman's matted hair that's strong as a rope,
beside the jangling man with dazzling teeth,
that ample turbaned gentleman, tent knee'd.
Or there—the blonde who got up, turtle broad.
You're watching how she walks: a turtle stroll.
Street vendors hawk their chilly for a dollar

by storefront mosques, past Orthodoxim stoles.
Playing with Big John and Ken at school,
you'd make a perfect spectrum, light to dark.
From Nordic white to sleek mahogany,
my Mediterranean Jew, you are the middle
figure in those colors' tri-tone scale.
So tell me, little Man, what should I say
to you who stopped that giant eight-year-old
cold as he was climbing up the fort,
when you shouted down at him,

"No colored boys allowed?"

PRIDE DIARY

1

Who knew it's quite all right that I downed three
gin-and-tonics (can't fit male inside
female part on fanny pack) at four
o'clock the Dyke March day of NY Pride?
Who knew Manhattan streets would liquefy
and lurch with dames sans bras, sans hair, sans shirt
in step with beer-can band led by a skirt-
ed trans in green brassiere, led by the cops
whose sentries are staid as posts with glasses on,
lined up beside the march like S/M tops?
(They seem to think Gay Pride's this weekend's yawn.)
(Pit stop at McD's, can't clip pack back on.)
Who knew she'd march beside me hand-in-hand
and who'd expect me to remember names
when Liz's girlfriend saw us and waved "Hi.
It's... Anna"? (CNN shot feed, then frames.)
Booze-stymied by the glare of girls and sky,
how could I choose? Should I grip hand, or pray
wondering: Is today today the day
she'll let me turn the key, lead her inside?

2

Okay, I'm sober now. Today is just
the kind of day she talks but feels no lust.

3

Beside her isn't bad. Fan-stirred, the air
is humid and the theater is packed.
An ear-cuffed thespian tries to fix the cold,

our leading ladies sweat it out in back.
A prim man to my right begins to sneeze.
My nose is in agreement. The perfume
from Queen Mother there could clear the room.
This shadow play across her face is fine.
Her arm's near mine, which means exactly nothing.
Hope's hope hums on through separate listening.
That skull, opaque to me as Midland's vault,
her silky crop, its pepper dabbed with salt—
I chuckle at an apt sardonic line.
Her suede complexion, lifts up, checks the time.

4. LES NOUVEAUX FROM LA NOUVELLE JUSTINE

I don't love her. She doesn't love me. Neither
does this waiter who may think it strange
when young girls dine with staid dames twice their age
on *salade de Bastille* and *pain de Sade.*
I don't like sitting by her like wet cloth.
I don't like restaurants whose queers pawn sex
to the bachelor bunch who want a thrill.
I don't like dining with my, well, not-ex,
both measuring the humid air for signs
of sparks I see by parts will not ignite.
I'd rather have a knock-down, drag-out fight
that cleared the joint than watch another guy
get spanked by Corset Kris, who'd like to grab
a tit, not spend hip humping hairy thighs.
I'd rather I were twice *her* age and wise.
I'd spin cruel stories of past days of bliss
then give my own hands covert exercise
and send her home to bed without a kiss.

5. L'ADDITION

30 for the play and 10 for gins,
10 for two cabs and 40 for the eats,
at least the metro home was freezer-cold,
at least the Broadway Local still had seats
at 96th, the local went express.
I blistered home ten sockless humid blocks
back to my solo digs for solo sex.
I got this poem for my 90 bucks.

Who mind loved would not rather be loved body too.
Since all is all. Want eyes through everything. Like
comb through hair. Like water washing gold. Who
mind loved would not rather love body to body since
all is more than map making map that looks like man.
Who'd mind love. Who would rather love mind when
body needs body. Wants swing. Wants stone.
Wants flesh. Wants glass. If minds love (must love) (do
love) why not bodies love also. If not you who. Why
wise the uncertainty.

UNREQUITED LOVE

It's not so bad, really. This
moonshine without a flower. Nights
her breath is damp on your nape, her hands
on your hard nipples, though she sleeps
soundly, ten, a hundred, a thousand
miles away. She demands only
subtlety about the honey and salt
that flashes up

at you through the windshield
in the sleek exigence of acceleration,
thinking, *These are the words
with which it might begin,*
imagining this as the situation:
There is not a common
glass of wine on any table. Morning is
the spicebox of a day she might be in.

Get up. In the mirror above the toilet,
your hands ask for the person
they know you could be to drive them.
Your body picks its clothes, hoping
to end bared. After all, hasn't she
already gathered up the stories
of your life like a vase containing
the whole field? It would only take
the right light to make you shine.

Days can ache this way for a long
time. Your solitude, edgeless, polishing
sensation. Your mind engaged
like a new machine in the engine's traveling
conversation. In the oasis of a storm

channel, your favorite glove
in the muddy road. You stop. Then on
through the chosen passage, your shadow,
altar/image, stretching not toward, but up.

Four red sarongs, a wood horse from China,
sedulous chanting of drums, color, smoke.
Taste the corn roasted with butter squirted
from a mustard tube, the lemonade icy,
a glass of sun. Extremes of mind, temperature,
geography brought into the Sunday jostle
of packages and dogs. Street bouncing. Is such Jello,
this vibrating, resplendent air. Alarms, loudspeakers,
the military sound of a city checking its sheer volume
of peopleness, breathing, being coupled, uncoupled,
bemobbed, singular, and fondling the merchandise
from other worlds. Far off on a table at home
I've left everything I thought I had to do:
a stack of books and of neat homogeneous clothes
that say nothing but their own names over
and over. But here: the press of people, a vegetal
happiness. And above the beloved rooftops, evaporating
Winter, ice, salt. The chimneys of nothingness.

LEARNING STICK

1. WITH HIM

Eyeing a dashboard high as the San Gabriels,
I shake that thing, that wiggly bulbous member
back and forth the way he showed me to
and drag it into first and ease one foot,
trading weight and trying to feel cues
to shift, give over. Close to me, his lips
(*Next time put the clutch foot down. Remember.*)
twitch suppression to each start and jerk.
My halting round the block is wincing work
for Man as Mountain, rigid sealed machine.
Arms in a sweat, my heart jazzed, every shove
curses the beast that moves then will not move.
Strained with will-to-please, here is my start:
locked metal box fueled by a nervous heart.

2. WITH HER

Humidity lifts us tense and intricate,
descanting out on fifteenth-century roads
with names I can't pronounce. Lame rental car
after the automatic one gets towed.
I stretch my legs out in the driver's chair.
She says, *I'll teach you. Yes?* Me here, her there.
Then every nervous motion meets a sound,
her farm-bred coaxing, soothing, settling down —
soon we are sliding over night-sheened stones,
Bruce and Joni on the stereo,
and singing. If I stall once at a toll
as police pull up, and if once more
I stop a workday morning bus' rush —
hey, it's just fine, we girls, we only us.

3. WITH ME

Into a rhythm ruled by *kgrrrr* and *bprrrr,*
vibration I am born of, borne by, seated
on the driver's side. The whoosh of heat is
respiration to this solo drive.
Winter ice, the mirroring of road
gives me back my face my face my face,
the sheen of headlights slicing as I brace
my clutch foot with my gear hand in one motion.
Driving's solitary, sealed, devotion
that pounds my thinking into engine grime,
detaching, reattaching, driving time
meets meditation, speeding, shifting, slowed,
responses to my body and the road —
lessons of my life I've learned alone.

Three

MOVING TO CALIFORNIA

My son runs to stand at the edge of the pool
in his snorkel, mask, and tube, then will not touch the water.

At the edge of the new school's new red rug,
his small palms sweat into my knees all visit.

Does he think he can stand on a hill, skis pointing down,
and beg Gravity to drop him slowly?

Does he think he can untie a helium balloon
and ask it, politely, not to float away?

There is a boat whose right oar paddles upstream
while the left one backstrokes steadily downward

every time I open my new phone book
then dial an old long-distance number.

"Can't he swim yet?" Amber asks me,
a mer-toddler diving in the turquoise water.

"Even my sister don't wear floaties!"
Two kicks, she's wiggling, held-breath, underwater.

He claws up the trunk of me to safety,
his arms vise my neck, his small feet spurring.

"Let's go now!" his round tube slipping,
beach towel dragging mud, as we climb to safety:

to the dry, high shores of our empty condo.
How can I blame him?

BATTLE OF WILL & EXHAUSTION,
MOTHER & CHILD

Two knights surrounded by dinosaurs
are cornered in the kitchen—all threat and bluster.
Action figures always act,
even as night tries to soothe them under.

I am the one who laid a nervous hand
on a child's exhausted threat and bluster.
The bunk bed creaks as the story settles,
as night's cool hand tries to soothe us. Under

a Seussian drone I am thinking, anxious,
about someone with a nervous hand.
Will he sleep? Will he sleep? When will he sleep?
The bunk bed creaks as the shipboard settles.

What is the myth of a woman alone
who's thinking through Seuss? Her thoughts are drones
serving a terrible queen of their own.
Can she sleep? Will she sleep? When will she sleep?

The toilet's crystalline drip and the ghosts
of the walls are a myth. And this woman, alone,
is a captain steering too close to the rocks
where the ocean is serving a terrible queen.

Up on the cliff of a Friday midnight
the toilet's crystalline drip and the ghost-
ly snore of the sleepy one riding his dragons
can steer this sad captain away from her rocks.

"Rock me to sleep," cries the wild girl at twenty
up on the cliff with a young man at midnight.
Far below, waves from the sea of Alaska
snore back and forth, filled with moon's breath and dragon.

Up on the cliff of a Friday's midnight,
rock me to sleep with the sound that the fridge makes.
Warmth of a tub, hole of a drain.
Memories sleep in the seas of Alaska.

Action figures always act
upon the cliff of a Friday's midnight.
Warmth of a bird's heart. Chill of a stone.
Two knights surrendered. The dinos snore.

ALONE ON THE NIGHT
OF MY SON'S BIRTHDAY

The choices are long since made.
So why do I unmake and remake them
like a puzzle that turned out
different from the box lid?
Last weekend,
I brought home from the market

two tulips and one pink kalanchoe
my son picked out, its mass of sizzling buds
a clown's crazy hair. I set them on
a collapsible table beside the logs
in the corner I'd left bare
eleven months. "Relationship Corner," it's called

in Feng Shui. Then I felt like the young woman
in Thurber's *Is Sex Necessary?*
who brings two bluebirds and a couple
thousand lilies of the valley into her hotel
room on their wedding night, thinking
this is how you make a baby. Now

my mountain view is floral, hopeful,
tamed. The tulips have already lost their
heads. But one clownish kalanchoe blooms on
from its little table beside the china cat,
logs at its feet. Four years ago tonight
I woke from a dream of painting

                                  landscapes for sale
in my abandoned childhood home,
to a belt of pain around my belly. When
the strokes came at five-minute intervals,

his hand on the small of my back,
he shuffled me down the elevator
to the car and drove,

toes curling, back arching,
sunny, sunny February
light off every mountain like
the glistened hollow sweetness of a bell.
I rode beside him, both hands on the world.
I felt, I fell, I felt, I was making

as he steered us into the traffic of an 8 AM
commute, like horseshoe crabs
piggy-backing into the waters off Cape Cod
on the first day of the universe.
Seatbelt on, door closed, pain coming
and going in waves. Our day.

And wherever he was taking me, my Charon,
my Cupid, my Father, Twin, Lover, wherever
he was taking us, that's
where I was going. I had no intention—
none whatsoever—
of getting out of that car.

Coffee still warm in that small bone
of a cup. The narrow line of sunlight
on a carpeted floor. Tenderness.
It doesn't take much
in the gray eye of a washed-out week.

Rain, strain, the whole mess drips
as if it had some other place to go.
("Mother don't leave me here.")
The hug through overcoats like a bell
that doesn't sound. Or was it

a stranger's finger on an untouched cheek?
It doesn't take much on a rainy week.
Sometime the temple in the chest
is all sunbeams. Sometimes it splinters
open. Sometimes it is a cathedral's

must and dirt, scent of disapproval,
moral in the air. Though the confessional's
open, no one's there. Without ears,
can there be relief? Without belief,
can there be faith? Or disbelief?

This liturgy is someone else's song.
It doesn't take much on a rainy week
to make you warm, or long
or remember, or grow tender
or forget, or regret, or get things wrong.

NOCTURNE

Unable to sleep at 3 AM
I open the front door and stand

looking at our rural sleepy street.
It runs like a long throat

into a tongue of the major highway.
It has not killed me to be lonely.

Over and over
friends say love should be simpler.

And in theory
I agree.

But one friend has a lover
whose retreats are perpetual torture.

Another brings with her
a lake of attention so deep it drowns her.

Are we not simple animals, clinging together
for warmth, food, shelter, the larger

patch of green on the leafy tree?
Our minds are huge and full of echoes. We

seem hideously exact
in what we enact.

Tentatively, day blinks open
like the neighbor's street lamp, programmed

long ago, when someone first thought to do it, cared.
And along the gravel road a way is bared

limned with coffee grounds, milk cartons, bread crust, dust.
And rumbling on the dark rim of consciousness,

the 6 AM dump truck, billowing, blessed
like the grass-heavy hem of a wedding dress.

CUSTODY OR VISITATION

I am still the woman you love. You are still
the man whom I married. But the house is gaping
with ghosts, and our son is ready to leave now.
Now I'm still the woman with ghosts, mother
you loved, child whom you married. And the house
gave birth to a son. And the son gave birth to
the woman. I am still the man with the coat.
You are still the ape with the apron. I am not
the ghost in your house. I am the body your body's
afraid of. Bodies crave consistency's succor. Bodies
seek a simpler moral. If I'm not the mind you love now,
then I'm not the limb you'll brush up to. Then I'm
surely the arm you brush up to but the strain
in the eyes, in the pullback. And our son is ready
to leave. Now I'm not consistency's succor. Will
you mother the mother you married. I am not
the son of a mother. You are still the ghost in my
house. Not loved. Not still. Still yet. And an other.

CANZONE

Last night, by my front door, my box of books
arrived from Amazon—*How To Do Your Own Divorce
in California* and two other books:
one on vaginal fisting, and the other book
"Kimba the White Lion," a video whose script formed
the basis for *The Lion King*. (Okay. One's a video. I lied. Book
me.) My son's books
don't know the first
thing about morality. But Kimba does. He was the first
creature I wanted to be other than myself, long before books
gave me Charlotte in her Web, the Amazons. Kimba showed me the fist
was not the mightiest organ. Rather the brain, though barely larger
        than a fist,

can be subtler and more effective. Fist-
ing (I know this from more than books)
is effective because the fist
fills the vaginal space like the head of a baby, whose fist
clenching and unclenching will tease a mother's nipple to embarrassed
        life, to divorce
from its role as sexual. Or not. Depending on decisions mental (not
        moral). The fist
can make breasts as tender as a pregnancy or a baby's fist-
of-a-suck. Which hurts. Make no mistake about it. (These basics form
the basis for all other oral and tactile and carnal forms
of pleasure whether mawed, mauled, sacrificial, superficial,
        penetrating, or, indeed, fist-
ed, and are at least at first
painful to one partner, though they may later feel voluptuous.) Just
        as first-

born children are notorious for being a mixed blessing. How *first*
you crack the egg, *then* you scramble it. Take fist-

ing. The first
time you come, you may cry, scream, bleed. A first-
page warning in *A Hand in the Bush,* my new book
on fisting, proclaims that a casual fist can kill. A first
chapter covers latex, safe sex, cautiousness. I hate this book. If asked
    by a new partner or a good friend, I would say first,
"Fisting is mental, not moral. Who cares how many fingers get inside?
    Divorce
teleology from terminology. Sex from sense." Divorce
one idea from another idea, one book from another, though they may
    at first
arrive in the same box like twins. Form
binds. Form combines. Form liberates. Form

a marriage and the stiff form
of all heterosexual culture will fall on you like starch. The first
love affair contains the form
of every love after. Is probably the mother. The form-
al principle states that symmetry is more beautiful than a lopsided,
    singular pattern. Yet Shiva bears a fist
on one side, a palm on the other. Perhaps opposites form
a kind of symmetry also. The singular form
of a woman is lush, bushy, marvelous. But a woman whose bankbook
has run low on funds, her home to be sold at auction, is booked
on the foreclosure form
posted in the foyer as "Ms. Myra Hill, an unmarried woman." So I
    wonder whether divorce
is truly un-marriage, or another thing altogether: Divorce—

a state of altered being, tranformational, like the trinity of ice, water,
    and steam. Divorce
me. Will I be an "unmarried" then? Formally single? Singular? The
    trick is not to form

needless connections in the first place, nor tense muscles you do not
    need to use. Divorc-
ing tricks the mind into thinking you can unscramble eggs. Diverse
sources say maybe you can. I'd like first
to try out divorce
from a perspective divorced
from civilization, unification. Clarification: Is the nude beautiful
    because we imagine a symmetry, a pair of eyes watching her?
    Her counterpart, a fist?
As if nudity were always in dialogue... I think I'll never fist
again, if it must be as the book
says: latex, safe sex, disconnections. I could write the book.

Marriage creates something larger. A fist
Is more than the bent bodies of fingers. At first,
It's a little like creating a baby: marriage forms
A third lifeform, an Us. Intimacy, also, is a book
Read slowly. A lover looking down at a lover's fist
Rising like a baby in her pubic cavity can hold the form
Of two (or one) long enough, to divorce
Here from now, there from later. Divorce
Is the word you don't write in Holy Books,
An arithmetic you cannot scribble with a fist
Of fingers. Divisible yet indivisible. An order of books
From Amazon. Why use more fingers than fit. At first.

Monastic

Work and the love a bare wall gives the eyes
when from one dust-free end-stop to another,
a single life's embraced parenthesis
is borne, belabored, breathed in over and over.
Sofas, tables, stuffed full-bodied chairs
slouch on fragile bones like former lovers.
Their surface skin is memory-stained brown
with watermarks of dusk through an open window.

I stare far off like my own childhood's widow,
where the fallow field of night is on the grain.
Letters peek out, folded into books.
And something not mine calls me on the rain.
Liquidness is lonely as a brook.
I married this. *Sum ergo Fido.*

Romantic

Sag paneer by take-out, pungent, sweet.
A flame sends pulses dancing out, makes stable
drumbeats through a single glass of wine.
Two rhythms partnered on the checkered table.
A distant conversation at the neighbor's.
Then footfalls up the alleyway. A cat
caterwauls a sexual brand of labor
over a wall I never intend to pass.

If I want to hear a personal voice here,
I'll have to lift the slim waist of receiver.
No mind will come to find mine if I don't.

I eat and let my eyes rest on the tome
of Brooks or Bishop open by my plate.
Wine lisps the meter as I contemplate.

Bacchanalia

Just drunk enough to spill a glass of wine.
Foggy capped, too numb to focus, feel.
What's the concept tangled up in twine?
Cast the line, pull on the tethered wheel.
Numb of metal heating. Numb of coal.
Pound, pound. Take on the soft. The smelt
and battered object standing in for self,
a stand-in while the other sits offside.

My second-rate pitcher, benched and overpowered,
must bide the tension as the score lifts, tied
while he may neither play nor hit the showers.
Tangled in my own limbs overgrown.
Tangled in my grown limbs, other-owned.
Deep in my cups, the cusp of inaction, whine.

Correlative

I once asked my friend Jiff
what a woman does in a house alone, as if
I could try on solitudes like dresses.
"It's hard. I got a dog," says Cris.
"I like to sleep with the TV on
for sound. Or else pick up the phone
and talk with someone," Gwen answers.

And also I remember drunken calls,
10, 11 at night from another
woman I'd wanted as a lover. Ella
crooning out winter from her stereo while I
hid for solitude in a closet to listen, my own
life rattling on without me upstairs: "I'm all alone
in this Big City. Oh Lady, be good," through the receiver.

Conundrum

Someone once said I spin
like a top over the soft dirt
of the day's subject, un-
til I tunnel into a hole, hurt-
led by stasis, inaction like a funnel
to the mouth of the matter
and can't get up:
my thinking carves a channel.
Something about mother,
this always wanting deeper
wanting back
up the vaginal tract,
a suck-a-thumb sleeper
weaned young to the Cup.

Vampiric

I am patently afraid of my own sleep.
If I had as much sleep as I wanted,
wouldn't I want more than I could get?
Only delay a little, the green creep-

ing numbers of the iMac's clock, haunted
but rising. Ether fills my head like rhyme.
Find another site. That's it. Chatter
clatters out from it's-all-and-everywhere time,
in the town, Virtual, where Lonely hangs
a shingle and Hopes tango under everyone's moon. Better
than dreaming, the Insomniac's fireflies flicker, passing
Fascination, Expectation, the Crest of Midnight,
and then it's AM of a day I haven't slept in yet.
Not enough dreamtime left before light. Not enough night.

1 a.m. —

But still I finger the wet and ridgy place
I am grounded to before
I try to sleep. God over the bed. I speak to Her. Or
I am an infant, swaddled, warm, turn face
and touch myself as namelessly as that
precognizant child. Sometimes other people
crowd around, and while
my Thought, helpless, watches,
I must be loved through chains.
Sometimes it's unthinkable to know
the deep foamy center of the matter
with my own hand, so I hold
a pulsing foreign Otherness to myself,
when it's most intolerable to be alone.

Matitudinal

And again dawn over the distant trees.
The veil slips from the body and I fight
every urge to stay as numbed and stunned
as a Crab poked by a Jellyfish of Light.
I ease into the rituals begun
to start again and again an ancient engine
while in the eucalyptus—a convention
of sparrows. Orgiastic shifts in key.

This life I've written out and can control
restarts in water, purified and clean.
Then coffee, mantric, meaningful, and whole,
to sip out on the patio in the keening
sound of a day that calls me back and in.
The stony path through anywhere is Me.

A HIGH COLD BRIGHT FULL MOON

And it hasn't happened this way for 133 years!
December 22, 1999

Had I climbed the mountain where women find tough
footing while this fistful of moon lifts glowing
over Griffith Park, now my climb-worn voice would
reach toward the others.

If I'd loved a man who loved stony midnight,
we could drive our son to the tops of mountains,
let him sleep in back while we parked and stationed
eyes up toward heaven.

Clutch down. In the street I will never live on,
sound stops. And my little one clicks his seatbelt
off and wiggles out from his nest of cushions
in to see father.

Am I really one who has found her footing?
Will I speak my mind to demands that anger
me, or answer back to the soldiers waiting
with the wrong orders?

I'm no longer anyone's perfect daughter.
I'm no Jewish matriarch of a long chain.
(Watch me climb down mountains to keep my face in
family albums.)

If I spent the day in the pull of planets,
starting with my nose to the flowered mountains,
yellow-wistful, wanting to hold the faces
of moving people

while the tugging arc never let me reach them,
lifted off the light-and-dark homes I cherished,
I would surely raise this cold fist of moonlight,
tiny and angry.

Home, there is a roof where the moonlight settles
bluish, like the screen of a finished movie;
on the deck, white blasted, my apposite image —
Moonshadow's shadow.

When I hold my son in the early morning
(since he always calls for me near 4:30)
in my bed, his breath tugs my world like oceans.
Lose him, I'm tideless.

If I loved a girl, we might swim by moonlight
in the desert, following sulphur hot springs....
If I loved myself, I could swim by moonlight
into some other.

On the ground, my hands are the blue of lilacs.
In my chilly chest, lucid thoughts are arcing
out to meet trajectories of some other.
But I don't know her.

Up in Griffith Park, they have surely finished
gazing up, and now will reclaim their stationed
cars, turn on their headlights, sip canteen coffee,
steer themselves homeward.

Nippy air turns back all our astral gazes,
takes the charm from stars, meteors, and planets.
I would like to find out the place a moon can
come closer, lift free —

The light can only carve so much. The night
is a cricket-pressing darkness, a wet wool coat,
through the open screen, through the unlit rooms,

and my son, squatting in the light's circle,
shows me how he makes eight trucks go,
and then doesn't show me. His story plays itself
on the one-room stage our light's carved out:

Echoes of the stories I read him in his stories.
Echoes of the language I leave him in the night.
Echoes of the history I cannot say,

the ache of the body's want, the office day,
the papers in the clip on the unlit desk
and the tiny drama where they were left.
How language, simply language, sinks me;

how a workday "No" or "You" can make
my chest slope, my shoes feel tight,
my clothes ill-fit. But now here he sits

in his patch of light:
I bulldoze rocks. I cut the hay.
I wash the sand. I smooth the road.
I lay the tar. I dig holes deep.

I hum my mother's world to sleep.

I smooth the road. I like to grate.
I bulldoze sand. I lay the tar.

I dump my load. I drag a rake.
I sing my mother back awake.

I sing my mother back awake.

LETTER FROM HEADQUARTERS

What a day! The rat maze was lively. One girl
Got fired and two others bought a new car
On the Net. By 6 PM, my desk had its usual

Three paper cups with old tea bags and a soda can,
And an ether trail of guilty Web trips to procrastination.
Horoscopes, numerology. Today, I ran your numbers next to mine.

Casual games. They tell nothing personal. Only seem
Personal. A wish list. Or a mirror. Of fears or dreams.
At lunch, out on the last manicured patch of green,

I faced a hillside rough with California chaparral:
Yucca, those burnt-out mountain candles, a gray thatch
On their giddy stalks where once they were white with bells,

Seized by ridiculous blossoming. A jester's rod
Riding the spiny back of a hedgehog, its nose in the sand.
Now they are the shell of what they were. Dead—

They seem dead. Posts sticking up like markers
On a lightning-leveled field. They will bloom again
In spring (I have seen it before). Back upstairs,

I returned to the fluorescent sunrise of my desk,
Where I clicked and moved yellow trains of text
Across my screen. It's been so many weeks

Since someone touched me that when
Sun Lee laid a job bag by my hand,
That moment her forearm brushed my skin

Brought brandy to my cheeks
And lips before I returned to the tall singleness of my stem.
Most days, I like these solitary weeks.

The intimate corners of my intimate bed. Sundown
In a house with candles. My own hands
On my own breasts. My spirit nobody's but my own.

My thoughts, ditto. My spaces, self-arranged.
In this decade I will not share with anyone
But my son. How I have changed,

As I open the door on a dark room with no one there,
To wooden train tracks on the floor,
Last night's Batman mug on the stairs.

Wanting mostly to stay warm
On nights I dream of a woman tangled in my hair,
Or my own hand reaching in a burrow, finding shy life inside of fur.

Sometimes, my ex brings our son to my apartment door
And asks whether I would like something casual
All night. And I say, "No." Thinking to stay reliable for—

For what? For whom? Here the weather is implacable.
Yours waxes and wanes like a moon.
I do not want something casual

With you. But for five weeks, your dawn messages in my ether
Have made the sun rise, and I jump out of bed
And into my day's solitary adventure

With your voice riding shotgun at my side.
After work today, I stepped off the edge of grass and climbed
Up the dusty slope where beige lizards hide

In tiny holes, where the cactus are anchored like thumbs
Among the spicy sage and desert paintbrush,
Inside the brown-green tangle of shrubs.

And sure I could make some comparison
Between blooming yucca and hope. But I believe
It is a cycle, and I question

The urge to deliver, every few years,
The baby of oneself whole to a new home.
I am *so certain* I ought to live alone. But over

And over, I have taken the long road to the obvious.
I want to call this new way what it is:
How I am finding in sand, in dust

Enough for bloom, enough for sustenance.

GOING DOWN

for Erin

Full of our ambition
We climbed the fire-road
On a hot day
Above the herd of live oak
Grazing Strawberry Creek.

Looking down into those gnarled solutions,
We talked of hopes big and small
Until we came to a slope
Flaming with California poppy.

There you made me stop
While you bent down to touch
The silky purse of the poppy
With your hand

And stuck your nose so deep
Into the flower,
It must have reached
The Chinese tassel at the center
And grazed each pink-sheened surface.

Then you stood up smiling,
As if you had found the only coin
Either of us would ever need.

RIQUEZA

Tengo la dicha fiel / y la dicha perdida:
la una coma rosa, / la otra coma espina...
  Gabriela Mistral

Although the Eaton Wash was pink with ghost
and dust, I took the horsy path again
down to where the water and the rain
meet. My toes are happiest when placed
where specks of guppies cluster light and tumble
water on my skin up to my ankles.
Moss in brackish eddy rides the ripples.
Sparrows dart away from me like troubles.
Sagey, dusty, doggy smell of trail
drags my body back to what is real:
I have a faithful joy and a joy that is lost.

The night you flew twenty hours home from Oman, got
Sam to sleep, we sat on the kitchen floor,
blasted with a clear domestic light,
and I told you I couldn't stay married anymore.
We took our regal bands from our ring fingers
but yours wouldn't budge—knuckles outsized joints.
Was the Divine Jester making points?
Perhaps. We ended at the sink—in blood, cold water,
I holding your whole body from behind.
Although it didn't imply change, it implied,
I have been faithful, Joy. I have been lost.

Mommy, can't we have "old family" back?
I want you and my dad to live together.
Is Grandpa Andy really Daddy's father?
Are *hot* and *cold* or *east* and *beast* a match?
Why can't I make the video in my head

play only good dreams? Mommy, don't help.
Mom, you're the best mom in the whole world!
Look, I poured the milk out by myself.
Do you miss me when I'm at my dad's?
How come you have my helmet but not my knee pads?
I have a faithful joy and a joy that is lost.

Eaton Wash. I walked there with my love.
Eaton Wash. I dreamed there of another.
One who'd gnaw my insides like a bone.
One who'd tease my tears out like a mother.
One I wanted till my nipples milked.
Dusk spinning with life inside her room,
cranky, cunning, keen insightful talk
in that garden overrun with bloom.
Moments would expand there like a lung.
Raw, uncertain, realizing, unstrung,
I am unfaithful, Joy, but far from lost.

Echo the perfect conquest of the sea
over every groomed, tamed, patient shore.
Stitch a salvaged piece of what I've torn
into the quilt my son keeps on his knee.
Rich with purple martins, rich with sparrow,
live oak, flat bush, goldfinch, tufted brown
stream birds that dart off from me close to ground.
I am as rich with purple as with sorrow.
Thirty-one, an acorn, dropped, reborn,
resting on the dust (or stone) exhaust.
Oh how loved is the rose, how loving the thorn!
I have a faithful joy and a joy that is lost.

ABOUT THE AUTHOR

Jenny Factor received her bachelor of arts in anthropology from Harvard and Radcliffe Colleges in 1991, and her master of fine arts in Poetry from Bennington College in 2000. She has worked as a contract archeologist, a freelance writer and editor, and a writer for EarthLink. Her work on this book was funded by the 2000 Astrea Foundation grant in Poetry.

The Chinese character for poetry is made up of two parts: "word" and "temple." It also serves as pressmark for Copper Canyon Press.

Founded in 1972, Copper Canyon Press remains dedicated to publishing poetry exclusively, from Nobel laureates to new and emerging authors. The Press thrives with the generous patronage of readers, writers, booksellers, librarians, teachers, students, and funders — everyone who shares the conviction that poetry invigorates the language and sharpens our appreciation of the world.

PUBLISHERS' CIRCLE
Allen Foundation for the Arts
Lannan Foundation
Lila Wallace-Reader's Digest Fund
National Endowment for the Arts

EDITORS' CIRCLE
Thatcher Bailey
Breneman Jaech Foundation
Cynthia Hartwig and Tom Booster
Port Townsend Paper Company
Target Stores
Emily Warn and Daj Oberg
Washington State Arts Commission

For information and catalogs:

COPPER CANYON PRESS
Post Office Box 271
Port Townsend, Washington 98368
360/385-4925
poetry@coppercanyonpress.org
www.coppercanyonpress.org

This book is set in Sabon,
designed by Jan Tschichold.
Book design and compostion
by Valerie Brewster, Scribe Typography.
Printed on archival-quality Glatfelter Author's Text
by McNaughton & Gunn, Inc.